To Hilda & George
with very best wishes
David

STRUCK

BY

LIGHTNING

Miscellaneous Verse

David Manson

Esmeralda Press
1999

Published by
Esmeralda Press,
12 Wheatley St.,
London W1M 7PS

ISBN 0 9536102 0 9

Printed by Imedia Print,
London NW1 7EP

Cover by kind permission of Sir Terry Frost RA

To my loved ones

CONTENTS

POPPIES

Before the tractors and macadam men,
hard-headed, decked in big checked shirts,
have quit the blue-black motorway
they drive new-laid on engined lines,
on banks of new-turned earth that once
lay decades deep beneath rank nettle, grass
and rosebay willow-herb,
now moved to face the sunlight of a higher
world,
thin-stalked and wide-eyed poppies stand.
And in the well-worked, ploughed and
furrowed fields of wheat,
heat-speckled, sudden poppies make a gay
display,
What drove them there?
What wayward tide had spilt the feathered
seed
precisely here or random there?
While in the fields of Passchendaele
profuse they grow from dead mens' loins,
all planned on maps that drew
the foolish line of trenches,
so marking fertile sites for death to strike
too soon,
and talent waiting for its birth in human seed,
thwarted and transmogrified.
Without the tearing of the earth,
without the scissored land,

without the killing would the poppies see
the light of day,
or lie forever still, dormant,
knowing peace in latency.

PLATO'S ESSENTIAL BULLSHIT

In thinking of the things I know,
those things I think I really know ,
I look around the things I see,
an apple on an apple-tree ,
and wonder if its round red presence
is but the shadow of the essence
seeded by thought planter Plato
beside a necessary potato ,
prospering in an Elysian orchard
(or are my thoughts a little tortured?).
I wonder if such mundane things
as mud and dirt, mosquito stings
have essences of higher being
much better than the things I'm seeing.
Of all the animals that I know,
Let's take that angry beast, rhino;
it's hard to credit it's a mammal
but let's face it, so's a camel.
Do these horned and humpèd creatures
have essences as Plato teaches?
Does an a priori dromedary
on a priori sand make merry?
I find the notion very queer, that
there's an out there and a here.
And as for symbols on blackboards

I find maths thinking very flawed,
that numbers live on higher plane,
both essential and mundane.
Give me philosopher, Dr. Quine,
I find his thinking same as mine.
"A thing is not an entity
unless it's got identity."

VINES IN MAY

Prancing, dancing girls,
the vines in May,
bobbing in their pea-green hats,
Merlot, Pinot Noir and Cabernet.
Earthbound chorus pruned and rooted,
hobbled on arthritic feet,
twisted witches stand black-booted,
whisper on the Gironde wind
sorcerred spells of fermentation,
vendange , pot-stills, distillation.
Les madamoiselles de Chardonnay,
sans entrechats and pirouettes,
brew ancient potions of regret,
blazing stars and Saturn's rings
that dance and prance in agitation,
parody the girls of spring.

STRUCK BY LIGHTNING

All told my life was penny plain,
the pavement that I trod was flat,
my settled road reflected light
but only on the days it rained.
Trapped in a cage of red-tiled roofs
stretched to a tight horizon,
I knew an appetite that gnawed,
I felt a vacuum at my soul,
a space impossible to fill,
an empty plate, a meal spooned thin,
my stage a scraped-out porridge
bowl.

There was no warning in the air
alerting me to what might pass,
no shot, no horn,
no thunder clap.
a sudden haze of violet light,
a yellow slash so sharp, no pain,
a massive jolt,
a shattered glass,
and when her shards had struck
my breast
the prism of my life had changed.

SO WE LANDED ON MARS!

This humble bee, that silly rabbit there,
we put them somewhere on the list
above the worm, soil-turning food for birds,
who rank on high, but are they higher than
mankind, the animal that God has blessed.

I see mirrored in this friendly canine's eye
myself, but what I wonder does she know
of me?
Some kaleidoscope, perhaps of colour, smell
and sound in frequencies beyond my ken.
Will I ever know? I have no way to tell.

Puffed up we crowd upon a perch,
survey our cosmos through a clouded lens
and crow myopic cries of exultation.
We, back-slappers, pleased as punch,
drunk on pride and self-congratulation.

There is a world out there I cannot know,
not mystics' far-fetched fantasies, or those grey
offerings
that chalk-stained mathematicians bring,
but constellations dreamers know
on hearing melodies that only angels sing.

What I do know – but know is not the word –
is small and planted on that span
where there are lines, the measure of my
mind's geography
that counts five fingers to my hand
to bound the certain limits of my world.

METAMORPHOSIS

The pupa hangs at chrysalis,
immobile, blank-faced carapace.
No hint of hidden turmoil in suspense,
while memories of silly larval days
by ruthless phagocytes dissolved.
Seams strain and waters break,
it's all ordained.
There is no voice,
there is no element of choice.

Dear lady, why not step this way,
the coloured one's for you, I'd say.
So entering the mirrored box,
then curtain shielded stripping off,
she stands reflecting on her rounded flank.
Oh lovely woman, spread your wings,
imago stands for everything.
You have the choice, for fate is kind,
when gowned fulfil your need to fly
and leave your cubicle behind.

Where, I wonder, are my gaudy wings?
Where my vest, Adonis blue?
I'll wear my tortoise-shell cravat
when I am free like you.
My silver-washed fritillery,

a painted lady on my chest,
I'll fly, all nectar charged
and leave this hobbled world behind.
I'll soar on rising thermal air.
I'll leave this hollow world below
to breath at last,
to seek, to find,
and even if there's nothing there
I'll know.

A BLESSING

When you find time to put your dreams
to bed,
reflect on words in mind unsaid,
feel no regret for space that might appear,
for in my mind those words have come
so clear.
I, like you, regret the passing of the days,
you're here by me in many, many ways.
As time's remorselessness uncurls
I know the blessing of an evening-haloed
girl.

THE WARD AT NIGHT

No cairn or stele, Rosetta stone
could tell a tale as eloquent
as that tall column by the wall,
which silently declares its good intent;
not etched in enigmatic lines
that mask some studied mystery
but plain in black and white,
"I'm oxygen, the staff of life."
The element that found us all
through ancient fern, great canopies of trees
and silent forest exhalation.
All is quiet in the ward
where whey-faced walls
unblinkingly observe supine
but restless mounds that seek to find
the pulse of air that breaths behind the gasping mask.
There the column stands well-rooted on its trolley wheels
and there its single stem extends to light
the darkening platform of his mind
while spider-like his fingers cling
and grope to cling to anything
that might connect with memory
confirming life, and ease diminished lungs and weary heart
that centre on that good intent.

Then beside his bed he knows the turn of
engine wheels
and sees the round black face that fills his view,
the great express, not racing now,
but moving stately to its station
where soft-pressed buffers wait to make
the final touch where contact breaks,
the resting state that marks the end of line.
And there beside the wall the column stands
unmoved, for peace has come and all is silent
in the ward.

THE MOMENT

Never again to know the moment
and see the ocean's boiling spray
transfixed just there.
Just there in time and space
while seabirds swoop the curling waves
roll in.
Can the lifted water hit the beach again
like that?
Or drifting clouds repeat illusion as they
do just now?
A face dissolving angled jaw
drifts by to blink away fragmented
as a broken truth.
In shadowed green the sea
is patterned once and only once
like that.
Beach houses stand as they have stood
unknowing of the moment,
mute in multicoloured lines.
Time's arrow still, held still while
flying,
infinitely punctuated.
(Count the quanta you who know so
much).

Yet I have known this face
to hold the moment
and remain unchanged.

COCKLE-DOODLE-DOO

(With apologies to Isaac Bashevis Singer)

To you who see me chicken-wired,
simply known, a figure of fun,
mounted on my puny pile,
with twiggy legs and scrawny bum.
You see the carpet of my yard, my realm,
as messy straw and filthy grit,
pockmarked by scattered corn twice pecked,
know that I'm a cock and this my pit.
My tail still smoothly curving back,
not sparkling-eyed or peacock spread
yet proudly arched in shining black
If not for me, my clarion call,
your daily sun would not be born.
Just look at me, half-cocked I'm not
erect I stand and pistol drawn.
You see hang limp my orange crest,
but I defy your scoffing laugh,
at life's best games I am the best.
Acknowledge me,
a fowl deserving deference and envy,
and I'll reveal the story of my hens,
now only three but in my youth
I'd count them in their tens.
Oh joy, to hear them squawk in confirmation
of my prowess and their elation.

So partridge plump my fertile yellow,
keeps our quota up to scratch,
I can bank on her production,
she's the easiest to catch.
I love to see her wattles wobble,
make her comb once firm go slack.
She's my most obedient of queens,
when I crow she knows her duty,
incubates my selfish genes.

My stylish black, she has good taste,
alas she's often sad and cool,
a lovely portrait badly mounted,
sometimes makes me look a fool.
Her spurning shrouds the whole enclosure,
disappoints my best laid hopes.
I must contemplate her future,
while her flesh is soft and tender,
should I ditch her in the soup?

Now my third, my white, my best loved bird,
in whom I find complete repose,
with whom I share the quiet hours,
from whom all my contentment flows.
Like me she senses worlds beyond the wire,
and shares awareness of that mystery
that somehow laid us in this yard
and put me here upon my heap,
to deal my claw the best of cards.

So you who watch beyond the wire,
short-sighted, silly, thick-skinned scoffers,
think me laughing stock, an ancient rooster,
little know what life can offer.
For I am blessed as few men are ,
and this I want the world to know,
that's why I stand here on my heap,
and why I wake you from your sleep,
and crow, and crow and crow. .

ON THE EDGE

(for Terry Frost)

There is a line where colours strike
to form a voice that cannot speak
but ring so bright in consummation,
heave palpating blue as breast,
on the edge where worlds collide.
From the high board swallows dive
careless of a safe arrival,
those who dare the white-faced board
feel the edge beneath their feet,
find in air there's no retreat.
How to find the truth in wonder,
strip away the eyes' illusion,
reveal a site where cant will wither,
know red segments haunting space.
Not dancing tadpoles in deep water,
where mystic symbols echo death,
but life ethereal in yellow,
where red and green can ride at anchor,
where chevrons get their due reward,
where hanging moons receive ovation
where olives grow on orange trees.
There where rhythms leap in family splendour,
all is love in this landscape.

THE WARD AT NIGHT 2

The night is restful now
but for his prayer-like moans,
a mantra from some distant shore
that punctuates the quiet of the ward,
and coma'd dreams obscure the glow
that burns at nurses' station.
There is a presence in the ward
that flits across each huddled bed,
wings beat at random , chance selects
the chosen offer no dissent.
Will he ever know this self-same bed
again?
Will he ever see the only sky that's left
to him,
the heavens of the ward, inert, the plastic
tiles
stretched out in regulation lines
that march their way down corridors,
dilated arteries well lit.
His caravan proceeds by trolley wheels
through double doors that paragraph his
odyssey.
So urgently yet so lightly borne, supine,
now on sedate to where his midnight waits.
Did an eyelid flicker then?
A nerve cell register a ceiling tile
that figures as a waning square
which in remaining mocks his passing now,
reducing now, the shutters tight,

impervious, the black box sealed,
while in the ward a new dawn lights.

MINDSET

This is the plan, the blueprint for the day,
compass points are plotted, neural lines are
laid.
The helmsman locks the tiller, synapses are set,
pre-ordained conditions, all requirements met.
other routes are neutralised, other plans are
quashed,
every pathway tranquillised , any choice is lost.

In mind there is a motor driven at
a certain speed, a steady rate,
a pendulum dictates the beat,
allows no falter, hesitation means
momentum's lost, the plan betrayed
and moments of unmeasured rage.

When I work out my menu for the week,
mark down commitments, letters, friends to
meet,
count minutiae by the hour,
underline momentous things to do,
documents arranged and files to hand,
I'm safe, I know exactly where I stand.

If I could slip this harness, loose my tie,
and walk through time upon a swaying line
defying air hung over space,
and crack this mindset carapace,
I'd open arms and sing, and take to flight,
and dive to fill the void with light

WAGTAIL

When you walk, you dainty strutter
across my lawn or in the gutter,
notwithstanding lack of size,
you're so evidently big, streetwise.
From your legs by some extendage
do you have control of that appendage?
You can do it, little bird,
in other ways, or so I've heard.
If some ligament was wound
could you do it round and round?
Would gravity be defied
if you did it side-to-side?
Maybe that long and jerky thing
keeps time for when you sing?
Maybe tailwag is a greeting,
sign that wagtail friends are meeting?
Let's consider evolution
and its mode of execution.
I cannot find on Darwin's pages
that tailwag gives advantages.
Jumping up and dropping down
and nearly sweeping on the ground.
I wonder if by any chance
that funny movement does enhance
some crazy form of sexy dance.
Something aided your selection,
what it is evades detection.
Whatever purpose drives that movement,
keep it up for my amusement.

EMPTY HOUSE

The house is empty now and tidying is done.
No mark, no trace, no impress stays,
as though necessity commands,
"Expunge all hint of other days."
No crumbs of comfort lie about;
the walls observe a single shaft of light
in which the dust haze mocking dances
on the carpet clean as new,
that once lay crumpled and askew,
now the studied focus of the room.
Life's mess concealed, all tucked from sight.
All sign of pulse is stopped; all stain is
scoured away.
I hear a distant morning sound;
the vacuum cleaner hums its melancholy lay.

TURNING TIDE

The evening tide is scarcely heard
as wearily it laps the shore
and with a gasping sigh retreats.
Spent, the yellow sea irresolute
strokes a sand of empty prints,
stretched out, it dozes in a waning light.

Beside me stands a void where once agog
with childrens' voices charged so shrill
could overwhelm sad murmurings
that gnawed, a rat to undermine the day.
In recollection these remain though faint
but reaching fingers find an empty space.

Doling out its moments one by one
time, that penny-pinching Scrooge,
resisting blandishments for change
to rush or brake its measured way,
it makes us wait, we have no choice
for time is no man's slave.

But that was yesterday
before the beach grew rich aglow,
and day stretched endless into night;
when gala beat beneath my skin,
knowing I would never be alone,
a steady pulse restored, the surf now rolling in.

PICTURE SHOW

We kids sat in line at the Gaiety cinema
looking ahead to the flickering show,
restless, impatient for the lights to grow
dimmer,
cheeks swollen with bulls-eyes that slowly
grew slimmer,
while hung in suspension, Harold our hero,
witnessed by hundreds of folk down below,
open-mouthed, breathless, to see if he'd fall
as he clung by a nail to a skyscraper wall.
Then Oliver puffed while Stan Laurel wept,
and bad men fought for the gold they had kept
in a mine-shaft of cardboard on a Hollywood
set.
Now we rest on our laurels on the Isle of St.
Kitts,
or wear a straw hat in befunct Biarritz.
When I lie in the sun, hat over my eyes,
I find those old images etched on my mind,
and remember myself, that child in the line,
and wonder if ever I went back in time,
would I tell him the show is not what it seems,
focus the picture and ruin the dreams.

THE ROSE GARDEN

I walk beside the railings black and high,
small cathedral spires tipped with gold
that point to prayers unanswered, dreams fulfilled,
and keep against those ancient unrewarding cares,
the well-sown garden of my soul,
once nurtured by the one who is not there.

I walk and look toward the Rose Café
to see a dark-haired figure waiting there
and know a moment's glimpse that stops the pulse
but find illusion strikes unfair.
At an empty table someone sits,
someone I know who is not there.

Then by the waterfall cascading
sounds that bridge their way from foreign lands.
"When we were in Kyoto," drifts along the wind.
The voice is hers for whom I care.
By water splash I stand there heron still,
and hear the song of one who is not there.

And now I walk around the water
where deep-rooted giants unconcerned
stand nodding willowed heads, their tresses
sweep the surface of the shadowed lake,
while mandarin and swan, white-buttoned coot
call forlornly, "She is not here."

To the rose garden's trestled stands,
I look for Lovely Lady, Polar Star,
but find I'm mocked by Rosa Munda, there
where Albertine and Mol McGrady grow.
Where is my Ballerina, Beauty Queen,
my breath of life, my lovely dark-capped rose?

HIATUS

A minor drought.
Not a white mandible in dry sand.
Nothing to weep about.
Not a wound that waiting cannot mend.

A gentle melancholy,
scarcely the stroke of a cat's tail
close purring by,
affirming what there is to feel.

Just an interval,
an intake of the breath
between the breathing,
so airless even memory is still.

Then from a lilac sky
there is a gathering of pressure,
a tightening of skin around the brow
waiting for the rain.

NEEDLEWORK

This tangled ball all knots and ends
that lie in unexpected places
can never breath in harmony
nor click and clack to melodies
where simple rhythms sing of sleep
and spin a skein of cosy dreams.
This treadmill for insomniacs.
This mesh, no basket of delight.
This maze that makes the sighted blind,
where I have picked and plucked
and gathered yarn to disunite,
and spent a life untangling
the snags I spun in pupa days.
All efforts meet to fray the ends.
so baffled now my state perplexed ,
I find my garment knit all snarled
more lovely than a smooth-skinned ball.

ESMERALDA

(For Hannah, Cam and Ruby)

Esmeralda queen of the bees
big and fat with very thin knees
said to her servant, an elderly drone
"Get me my hair pins, a brush and a comb
I'm really tired of sitting at home,
we've plenty of honey it's cosy and warm
but isn't it time we went on a swarm.
It's over a year we've lived in this nest
I think that a move will really be best."

"Your majesty's wishes I shall command,"
said the elderly drone, his cap in his hand.
"The message will go through the usual channels,
the swarming committees advisory panels.
I'm sure your people will recognise sense
in pulling up combs and zooming from hence.
I'll send out the scouts, they'll fly by the sun
Buzz, buzz, happy bees, it's going to be fun.

The elderly drone looked out at the weather
then he ordered the scouts to gather together
"You bees," he commanded, " must find a new nest
where our lovely queen, who's given her best
can lay new eggs for the next generation.
Zoom forth in the cause of our beautiful nation.
A hole in an elm tree would be ideal,
fly high and let's see what your search will reveal.

Then the brave scouts all buzzing took to the air
  wings flapping, excited, but taking great care
to keep all together in special formation
they knew that they carried the hopes of the nation.
So they danced as they flew, the sun on their wings
over roads, over trees, over cowsheds and springs
then they saw an old oak tree, hollow inside
"Perfect!" they chorused, and knew they'd arrived.

Back home, Esmeralda received the good news,
she called on the council and heard all the views
of the drones and the workers, the young and the
old
who cheered and danced when they were told
to gather together and prepare for a flight
with all their belongings, whatever they might
need in their new home, the hole in the tree
the ideal, the perfect home for a bee.

They combed their hair and washed their faces
They packed all their bags and boxes and cases
They carried their pans and kettles and pots,
their bedspreads and blankets and pillows and cots
They ran to and fro in a frenzy of hurry
some lost their tempers in such a mad scurry
then they all waited, their buzzing was low
until Esmeralda said," Bees, we must go.

Bees in a swarm make a big black cloud
the noise of their buzzing incredibly loud
In the centre the queen, incredibly slow.
The scouts in the front know the best way to go
so they swoop and they swirl as they fly through
the air
and they lead on the swarm as fast as they dare.
The sun has gone down when the bees reach their
goal,
and there in the field is the tree with the hole.

Once in the new nest the workers get busy,
their to-ing and fro-ing could make a drone dizzy,
and poor Esmeralda, she lies in her cell,
she's weary and tired and doesn't feel well,
her fat body throbs on her little thin legs
she's heaving and quaking and laying new eggs.
She isn't as strong as once she has been
and soon there'll be born a lovely new queen.

Esmeralda is fading, she's going to die,
her night is approaching, her day has gone by.
She calls to her helper the elderly drone,
"Bring me my hair pins, a brush and a comb,
I've worked very hard and now the job's done,
I'm off to bees' heaven, a place in the sun,
and a queen bee in heaven must look her queen
best," Then breathing a sigh she laid down to rest.

Esmeralda has gone
but we won't ever forget her,
she was a fine queen
and no queen was better.

MEMORY 1

In the tunnel of my mind
where shining neurones lay in lines synaptic,
interwoven, charged, their pathways charted,
coding messages of hyacinth and rose,
of belle-de-nuit and daffodil,
traffic breathing harmony, repose,
when fragrances of rosemary and lavender
drift in from unexpected places
and raise the blinds on memories of pain,
on treachery found festering
in unforgiving ganglia lain;
Siberia in sensory receptors,
there the east wind blows.
Where once a coloured carpet lay,
forgotten winter days.

MEMORY 2

And now, on looking back,
I wonder which of all those sounds and sights
and smells that drifting by , will be remarked
and dignified as memory?
And which of all those pricks and knocks
that tell us what it is to live
will scatter on a careless breeze
or infiltrate and dormant lie?
I wonder in which corner lies
-if corner is a word applying to obscurity-
the water splashed upon the face,
the taste of countless cups of tea,
and those events so many and mundane
that touch the skin but stay unmarked?
There are events that skating by
leave but a shallow line
that's quickly sealed and knitted over,
traceless as a passing wave.
Once planted, moments, sights and sounds;
the recollection of a finger-tip upon the cheek,
or hair that's ruffled carelessly
or gently smoothed, can prosper in the mind.
Such primroses of memory, that bloom
and on occasion richly spiced,
when fancy lit, and marked by smiles
or twinges of regret and pain.
And what of those so deeply etched
there is no chance of sound repair,
that stay a mark upon the face,

along with other scars that celebrate
quite who we are,
and how we came to be ,
in memory...

SHE

Pity the man that cannot know
the sound of your voice or curve of your brow,
and gentle kiss those shuttered lids
or stroke, soft finger-tipped
across your waiting nose and mouth
and down the pillar of your neck.
White crested shoulders, smooth and still to touch
invite that welcome slope to where soft nurture lies,
twin fawns of ancient Hebrew king,
so proudly tipped for play and comforting.
There stay awhile
and dream of cradled lullabies,
to wake in hollow bed
of arched pelvis open spread
where dimpled belly, soft and slack
domes down to firmer ground,
there to sip in shadowed tendrils,
tangled blackthorn now divided,
where two perfect columns white and still
sighing yield at pressing need.
There you lay, in touch and sight and smell,
known well,
and yet a girl unknowable.

THE FUTURE

The future lies in waiting, silent
in deep grass.
no trodden earth, no broken stem,
no telling odour on the breeze
gives hint of any menace there
to turn intention from its path.

Departure lounge, in limbo now,
the moving walkway left behind,
commitments in another time.
It's done, no options wait
and resignation marks the tide.

Like the sunset red, surprised
to find itself again renewed
when rising from its cock-crow lair
it mounts the day's expectant arc
and leaps loose bridled in the air.

So rubicund, the smile so broad,
a thick pale finger beckoning
our friendly publican awaits,
his parlour warm with red veneer
but hazard haunts his fake handshake.

A dappled dray-horse heavy-set,
its wagon skewed across the day,
blinkered, grazing unconcerned,
all destination screened from view,
as ever-present blocks the way.

The future is a citadel,
for lotus eaters there to find
in vegetation lightly mashed
lurk prophesies of paradise.
Up-end the cup and turn it twice,
Look warily, the future's blind..

MYSTERIES

Out there where Ursa Major points the way
across that firmament of light
and constellations dance to tunes
piped out by Saturn's rings and tidal moons;
there in the spangled ceiling of the night
lie mysteries beyond my sight.

On this Earth are untold other folk
who pray to gods in stone and tree
and know a world where fishes fly.
They feel with me time's pulse pass by
yet rooted in this earth like me
they know a world I cannot see.

My neighbour sits behind our wall
and shares with me a hedge of thyme,
of honeysuckle, lavender and lime.
Our common lives lie seeded in this soil
yet past his eyes lie nebulae
and worlds of mind I cannot see.

She who lies beside me parallel,
known to me in every crease and curve,
she who writes the stories that I tell,
who speaks to me without a word,
my love, who daily casts her spell,
she, my sphinx, by far the deepest well.

THE VULTURE

The vulture sits upon my back
as other gluttons of its kind,
its filthy scabbard of a beak,
knows no compassion, gouges deep
at ulceration never healed,
to feed upon the garbage of my mind.
Those dogs of envy, hate, mistrust,
snap at my heals, corrode my soul
make resolution into dust.
And jealousy, the claimant of what I scarce
possess,
snaps ravenous at gentleness and love.
These plagues diminish me
and make me less than I would be.
No scar or keloid mark the skin,
no blister of that mole regret,
which undermining certainty
make futile what once was built so high,
so purpose-led with joy and hope
that then could hold me tightly bound,
defend me from my own undoing,
ease me from the treadmill of my mind.

CROW

Arrogant, sharp-nosed, beady eyed,
black as coal and stuffed with pride.
Brilliantined each smooth and shiny feather,
crow, satanic dandy, tough as leather.
In the rookery there's a rumour
that you have a sense of humour.
To me you seem a troublemaker
with complexion undertaker.

Bionic bouncy pogo-stick,
backward leaning, not so quick,
hopping, pecking round your patch
you're not a pretty sight to watch.
When you lumber to a tree,
joining raucous chorus rookery,
philharmonic cawing choir,
makes me wish you'd all expire.

If I were scoring your I.Q.
there'd be no birds, or very few,
would get a score as low as you.
Compared with magpie, swift or wagtail,
by any test you're bound to fail.
In my hierarchy of the genus,
in carnal terms you rank as anus.

When I consider haut cuisine
and ponder on a coq au vin,
partridge, grouse, red currant jelly,
turkey breast on tagliatelle,
woodcock, pheasant served with quince,
par-boiled pigeon makes me wince.
When thinking of the birds I know
I quail at thought of eating crow.

A PUZZLE

How can I reconcile myself
to being one of many
moulded all according to my kind?
Such a multitude of selves defies
negotiation by my mind.
Each of us so transient, so easily displaced,
in fleeting memory so easily replaced.
But looking down I see that I am planted
in this place,
and I alone the one that cannot see my face.
I look upon the world of others not myself,
who, each in turn, see me
and in me see themselves.
Each flower stands alone, without connection,
singular among the many single stems,
while I need reflection to recognise myself.
Without this shape my puzzle's incomplete,
yet fitting in I ask, Am I subsumed?
To play my part am I unwittingly consumed?
In paradox I light upon the truth,
being one and one of many,
particular and part of whole,
twice am I made,
in connection and alone.

THE LIBRARIAN

Little John, hugely well read,
always took books when he went up to bed,
borrowed at least four books a day,
which prompted the other boys to say,
It can't be the books that he's mad about,
it's her that dishes those books out.

Little John said, What you say is so true,
if it weren't for that girl, I'd borrow few
books, perhaps none at all,
but she is adorable, lovely and small.
The library visit is merely a cover,
I borrow books because I do love her.

The library building became John's shrine,
on his library card he wrote, Please be mine.
He stayed awake most every night
and read six books by dim candlelight.
At dawn he waited at library door,
but one day found he couldn't see her any
more.
The place seemed empty, sad and strange,
she'd done a library exchange.
But on a board, white chalk on black,
a note said, Worry not, Johnnie,
I'm coming back.

THE LAKE

I recall those salad days when we,
sometimes two and sometimes three
friends
would circumnavigate the lake
and talk.
Constant talk of who and what we are
with passion and repeated pauses
on the ways of God and final causes.
Of Locke and Hume (whoever they may be),
then thirsty , hungry, home for tea.

Where once a lake a dark depression lies,
of gaiety there is no sign.
The lake is drained,
where had been growth in fertile ground,
go green with hope and expectation,
is desert, burnt sienna dry.
Residences, or so they're called,
clone in sterile lines
along a crest that once gave sight
to joy and flying aspiration.
Certainty there is, that's cynicisms core
that shutters out the light
for me, but what of those
who calculate a different score.

Six percent's a splendid deal,
bricks and mortar, they are real.
Three beds, a loo, a sunlit lounge,

a garden for the kids to play,
a dog, a cat, a welcome mat.
By fifty I've no more to pay.
I'd beg and borrow, steal and scrounge
to get a deal, a home like that.

I recall those everlasting days
when we, just you and me,
would take a boat across the lake,
and never talk .
In breathless silence, skimming eye ,
ahead the island, now a dusty mound,
tufts of clover, yellow headed broom.
Why must time mock and aspiration doom?
those innocents; from here that's how we seem,
but cannot live to mourn what might have been.

THE WALL GAME

When I recall that patch of dusty grass,
convolvulus and rose bay willow herb,
speckled scrub of buttercup and dandelion
that parachuted promise in the air,
There, chipped kerbs worn over years,
meridia of broken stones,
I know the rhythm of my father's youth.
I feel the beat of rubber balls
that beat against a wall so thin,
the tympanum of neighbourhood,
and with each pulse I call up Rose,
and Ginger, Jack and Four-Eyes Jones,
and was it Bess, the best catch of us all?
Right now, who is there that's left to tell?
I find them all, yet one by one,
as though a jigsaw fell upon the floor.
Yet from that barren soil,
well seeded by a deeper need,
we grew to comfort decked upon a lawn
where mower marks run straight and clean
to rhododendrons evergreen.
Pink lilies sway perfumed beneath a white
magnolia tree
where wallflower seeds were sometime sown.
So musing on that bouncing ball
I wonder on the pattern of it all.
Could there be bone in broken stone?

LOST IN SPACE

From my balcony I see,
suspended in mid-air,
cantilevered over fields,
green plumed these hectares fair,
that foreign crop defines the fact
my bedrock is not here.

That hamlet lying low, still roofed
sits there in clustered peace,
though centuries have passed it by,
light-fingered winds of time,
while reaching out I search for space
that I can know as mine.

Those lines of green sit parallel,
the wide horizon in their sight,
by copse of oak and stand of elm
they know the end to which they run,
while I perplexed am lost in space,
my journey but begun.

How will I tell, how can I know
which piece of land is mine?
Is there a sign I'll recognise,
is there a call I'll hear
that says, this is your house, this is your space,
stay still, your home is here.

SHAVING

My father scans a well-lined face
and sleepy-eyed surveys the zygomatic arch.
He cocks his head, negotiates
the mandible's sharp angle now defined
demands a careful turn of blade,
in the mirror as I shave.

I tilt my head, scraped clean of youth,
and watch him pull his upper lip,
a pursed complexion of disdain
that bristled clear beneath the skin.
Dismay I see and saw, regret and pain,
and now reversed I'm seeing him again.

It's all a case of balance, he would say,
sideburns symmetrical, sharp cut.
His fingernails met every obligation.
Standards, boy, he looked above my head
and recognised horizons that I failed to see,
no matter how I turned and stretched the skin.

There in the column in the neck,
that pedestal of high accomplishment,
beat twin conduits of life,
muscle screened in the mirrored deep,
so vulnerable, they challenge me,
old man, to rid myself of you.

AN ORDINARY WOMAN

An ordinary raincoat, belted, grey,
a knitted bonnet, red and gay,
possibly bought at a charity shop,
sits slanted jaunty perched on top
of hair carelessly brushed, drab brown,
to her sloping shoulders hanging down.
She hurries purpose on her face,
but with a certain elegance and grace.
I see she's heading for the District Line
which by good chance is also mine.
As usual the train is late
and standing side by side we wait.
So from the corner of my eye
I take the opportunity to spy
upon the details of her face.
of prettiness there's little trace,
but wrinkles round her eyes that tell
of humour, tolerance as well,
and patience that is often tried.
Her undistinguished mouth is wide,
suggesting readiness to smile
with just a tiny hint of guile.
Oh happy man whose fortune is to lay
with such a lively lady every day.

QUESTIONING

The morning star, the guileless child,
who looks unclouded on a world
that lies undimmed by cast of mind
or questions begging false response.
Inquisitive, demands a sight of level ground
and soil to which the truth is bound.

Inquisitor behind his desk,
his spotlight shines indifferent, lukewarm,
its stream is innocent, unknowing of intent;
the lens that concentrates transforms,
its focus sets the searching beam alight
to sear with that flame contempt
and spill the burnt black grass of guilt.

Old soul, terminal and querulous,
who lies in need of comforting,
resigns all hope of trust when eyes don't meet
and truth evades the lips that move
tomorrow's plans as though the sun must rise
for everyone, when memories of yesterday
throw shadows only on the wall.

Facing left, its mouth agape,
devouring doubt, the question mark.
It stands, an amber light that contemplates
a change of state, a crossing place
where angled stones of ignorance
give way to what? Can it be certainty,

that marshy ground where answers lead
to further doubt.
An endless chain where light returning
turns from evening
to the morning star.

DAILY BREAD

On the corner of the street,
her empty basket dropped at pavement end,
she feels the pressing need to linger
and stoop to feed her pigeon friends.
Pale blue in anorak and jeans,
the colour of the mangy birds,
she, the host of daily bread,
they, her flock that gather round.
What wings them there when she arrives?
Perhaps it's knowledge of a kind,
or instinct sharp as pencil point.
Just as the mainspring of a clock is turned
and tension breaks the striking hour,
they come as though a lesson learned.
While she, how does she tick?
How does she work?
What mechanism weighs to drive her there?
Perhaps the need to fill her day
with something purposeful and fine.
Perhaps the need to forge a bond
with something sentient and warm.
She stoops, but hardly any way,
she knows no measure of degree in bending there.
All is level in her mind.
The birds in winter need to feed,
while she, good fortune, she has bread.

ON THE JOB

I would, if I could,
live in St. John's or Chorley Wood,
but as things are, it's no real loss
for me to settle for King's Cross,
in many ways a better location
for someone practicing my vocation.
Transition time's a critical measure
that leaves an hour or so for leisure.
Throughput is the technical name
when all the clients look the same.
There isn't time for discrimination
if one is servicing half the nation.
It's very important to meet the need
to do my work at very high speed.
I take no plastic, only cash,
to take a cheque is really rash.
One always works by certain rules
and every trade has special tools.
What I do - I should confess ....
but think a bit, and try to guess.
I mustn't keep you in the dark.
I'm a railway station booking clerk.

MISSING PIECE

It gnaws away, I fear,
this need for you,
and missing you
I feel a stranger to myself,
my shape is not the one I knew ,
as though a puzzle almost done,
the centrepiece lies lost
the part that makes the picture whole
it seems mislaid, not gone
but laying hidden from my sight;
and fear I feel in case that piece
could easily be lost for good,
impossible the puzzle put to right
and unfulfilled that need
devours my day, cuts out the sun,
to blanket all my hope and all the light.

REGRETS

When I think of all the things I've missed,
all the mountains never climbed,
contemplate the girls I never kissed,
experiences of every kind,
I run to see my therapist
and empty all the contents of my mind.

But when I lie on his settee
and look at his distempered ceiling,
try to focus on the inner me
and vocalise the things I'm feeling,
I get this awful urge to pee,
eject those cups of warm Darjeeling.

He explains that feeling of distention ,
tells me that it signifies
all my urges in retention
and need to expiate my sins and all those lies.
But I say it's innocence creates the tension,
a few more sins would make me wise.

THE ANGEL

Death is the angel on my shoulder,
unhaloed, wingless, always nudging,
urging me with endless tales
of what could be if only I
could see as clearly as she.
And when at last she blows the wind
of words
into my lungs and lets me speak,
I hear me say that I must learn to fly
and be as colourful as you,
and take on hues that shine
and glisten in the air
as prisms breaking water do.
Now flying still, well compassed
by her touch,
with signs and words so soft at times
I cannot hear their tone but feel
astonishment,
a never-ending awe at what is meant
by what my guide points out.
She knows what I, and we, can never
know,
but if you let her share the road,
though wingless you will fly like me
and see through mists of unbelief
a hidden truth,
that death can never be an end,
it opens all the doors to life.

ON LOOKING BACK

On looking back from where I stand,
and turn to face the way we came,
from who and where I am to then
my starting point remains obscure
for time has firmly folded back,
collapsed, a mindless paper chain.
And even then the edge was out of sight,
only expectation, hope we knew,
those smoking ringlets in the air
that rose from kitchen schedules pencil
sketched
while fancy ran concentric rings
drawn precarious askew,
allowing us to float unanchored, lost, adrift.
That said, not all was built on unlined maps.
We started out with texts we knew;
visa, toothbrush, papers checked.
The road we planned was cut and dried,
but somewhere drifted off the track.
Without a compass suffered wind and tide,
and piloted by envy, jealousy and pride,
and chance,
that slip of tongue that caught the eye;
meridia drawn on mindless lines.
Kaleidoscopic moments brought us light,
metronomic movement swung us back
and hope was halted in its tracks.

In looking back from where I stand,
still not certain who I am,
I turn to face a phantom space
where merciless the wind of time
blows obdurate, in single file, unwise,
the only way it must,
from rosy dawn to lilac dusk.